# How to Make Money on the Internet without Investment

## A beginners' guide to make money from home

- Santosh Mali -

Disclaimer

All the material contained in this book is provided for educational and informational purposes only. No responsibility can be taken for any results or outcomes resulting from the use of this material.

While every attempt has been made to provide information that is both accurate and effective, the author does not assume any responsibility for the accuracy or use/misuse of this information.

# Table of Contents

# Preface

Welcome!

Thank you so much for buying this book. I know you will find it to be full of tremendous value. I want you to know that I do not take your purchase lightly.

In exchange for your purchase I am going to reveal to you some of the best ways you can bulk up some extra money working from home without investment even if you are a complete beginner who doesn't know a single word about Internet Marketing.

I stand behind these methods 100% and I am very excited to share it with you because I know it will work very well for you.

Before you continue reading this report, I wanted you to download this FREE Money Making report in conjunction with this book. You can download it here... http://freefinancialfreedom.com/download-free-gift.html

I recommend you download this FREE eBook before you continue reading this report so that you can know some extra moves with all the tips and tricks I cover in this book.

I will not fill up this book with a bunch of fluff. What you will get is only actionable steps that I personally follow.

Once you are done reading this book from start to finish, I have no doubt in my mind that you will know for sure that these tips and tricks help you making money from home without any investment.

All of the actionable steps in this book are completely free. You don't even need a single dollar.

The various methods in this book will work for you as it is working for other people. It will not work for you, only if you don't TAKE ACTION.

Alright friends, the way to get started is to quit talking and begin doing.

So, let's get started right now!

# Section 1: What Is Blogger?

Blogger is one of the favorite and free blogging platforms from Google available at blogger.com. It is always free and only requires your Gmail account to get started.

Before we proceed further with blogger, I want to highlight some benefits of having personal blog online.

Blog is nothing but your personal dairy on the internet. People love reading blogs on the internet and they quite believe in it.

On blog you can update your daily status, teach your blog followers what you know or what they want to know from you.

You can actively communicate and answer their questions on blog. You are helping them out for their issues. It builds trust among visitors and you can become an online authority over the time.

Now you can sell your own stuff on your blog. You can also promote or recommend the other people products or services (also known as affiliate marketing) on your blog and make some extra money from your blog.

So, let's get started with creating Blogger Account and setting up new Blog...

## Step 1: Planning Blog Theme and Keyword Re-search

First upon you need to imagine your blog theme and choose a niche [https://my.wealthyaffiliate.com/training/how-to-choose-a-niche] i.e. what kind of contents you are going to post on your blog. Choose something that interest you more like your hobby or choose topic that you can create content easily and frequently.

Ok, now you have imagined your blog theme. Now it's time to re-search some keywords according to your niche here https://adwords.google.com. Choosing low competition keyword(s) is good and profitable for your blog.

Once you logged in with Gmail account, click on Tools tab, then re-search for your blog keywords and note it down…

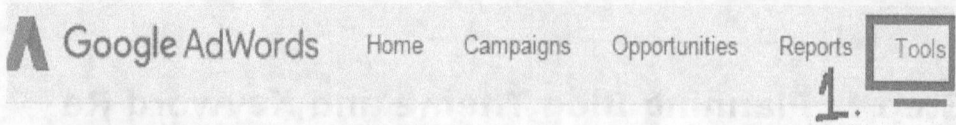

**Keyword Planner**

Where would you like to start?

Find new keywords and get search volume data

2 ▸ Search for new keywords using a phrase, website or category

**Click here to use Google's free keyword re-search tool**
▸ Get search volume data and trends

## Step 2: Creating Blogger Account and New Blog

Visit www.blogger.com and log in with your Gmail ID
and password. Once you have logged in to blogger
account, you will see something like this...

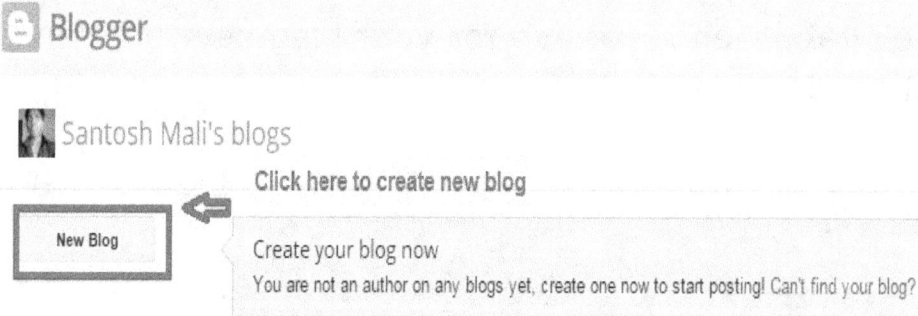

Click on "**New Blog**" button and following window
will pop-up to create your brand new blog online.

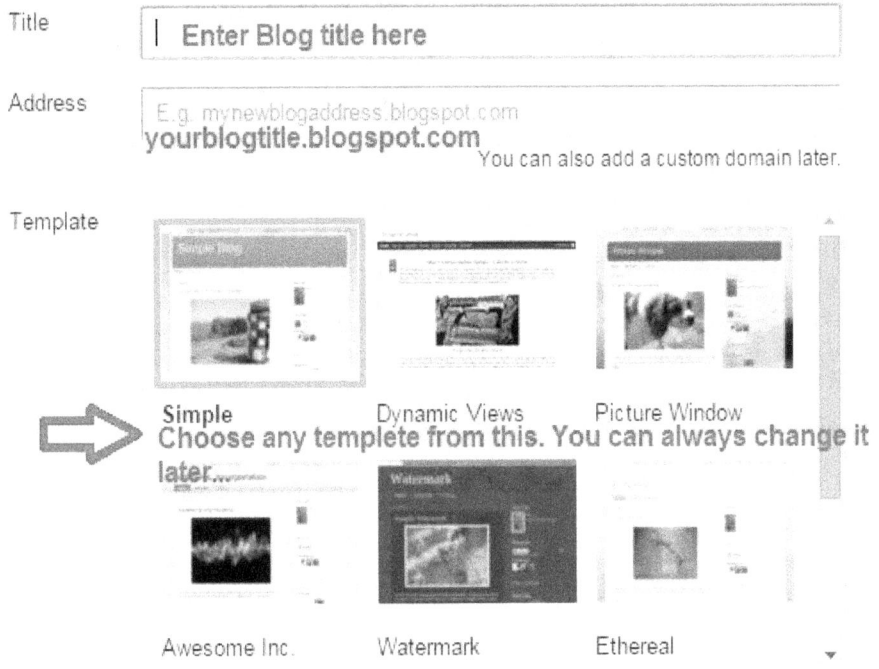

Enter the title for your blog (I always choose one of my keyword as a title for my blog and for URL).

Enter your blog URL. If the current keywords are not available for your blog URL, choose anything related to theme and easy to remember for your visitors.

[Having keyword in URL is good for Search Engine point of view. But according to the recent updates in various search engines including Google, your blog ranking will be decided on how unique and engaging your content is].

So, don't bother about blog URL. Just choose one easy to type and remember. Blogger is a free blogging platform so ".blogspot.com" come attached to your URL like "yourblogtitle.blogspot.com". If you want to use your own custom domain like "yourblogtitle.com", you need to buy it and then you can map it to Google.

Next, choose your blog template. You can change it anytime later and then click on Create Blog button as shown above. It will take you to the blog dashboard as show below ...

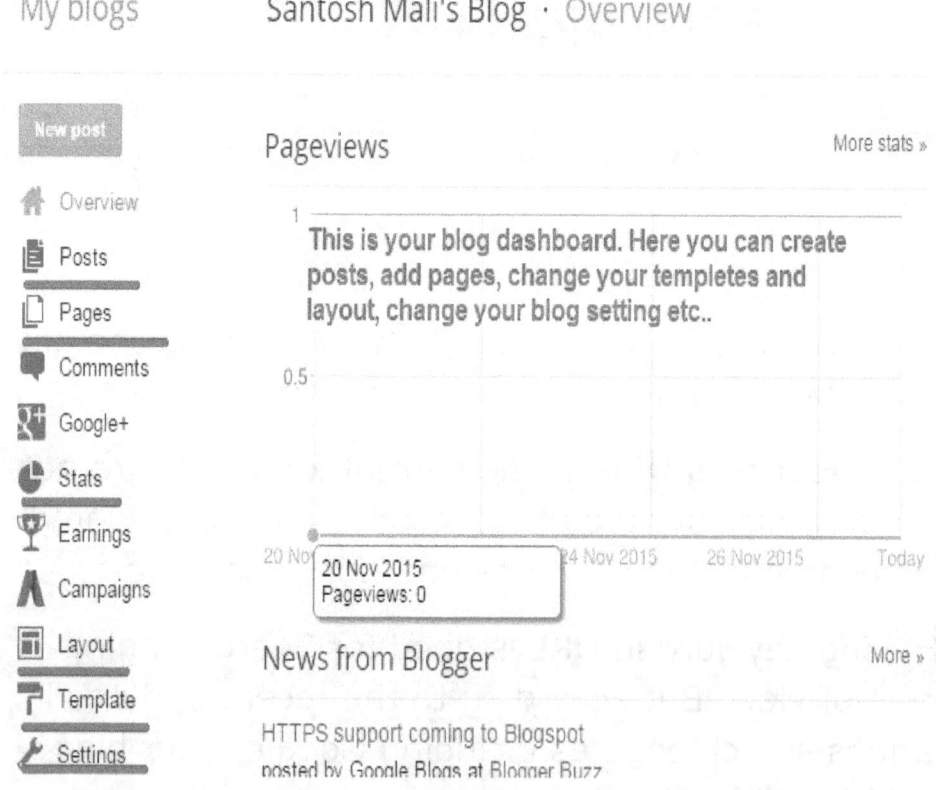

From this dashboard, you can create new post or page for your blog or edit it. You can change your blog template and customize blog layout also you can change blog settings anytime.

Go, click on settings, check out every link over there and edit whatever you want to change or update there and save it. And you did it. Your blog is ready for world wide.

## Mapping Your Own Domain with Blogger.com

Mapping your own domain with Google's Blogger account is beneficial for you, because you need not to pay for hosting your blog. It is free for life. But one drawback is that you don't have complete control on your blog. Google may terminate or deactivate your account without giving you notice if you don't follow their Term of Service.

Ok, Visit this link to know how to map your own domain with blogger [https://support.google.com/blogger/troubleshooter/1233381?p=customdomain&hl=en&rd=1]. Just go through it. If you getting problem setting it up, let me know at my contact details below. Here are three screenshots for your reference whilst mapping your domain name with above guide…

When you purchase a domain name from one of the domain provider listed in guide (I recommend GoDaddy), log in to your GoDaddy account and locate "DNS Management" and click on Manage DNS link as shown...

## DNS Management Free

► **Manage DNS**
Map your Domain Name to a Web Hosting or Email service, set Domain Aliases, etc

► **Name Server Details**
Required to use our DNS management service with your Domain Name

Once you click on that you will be taken to a screen like this...

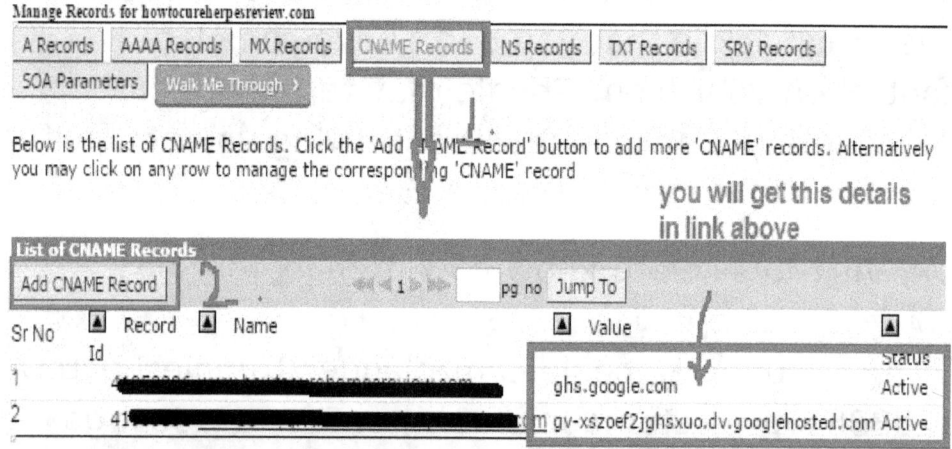

**Click on CNAME record tab**, then click **Add CNAME** record and Follow steps in guide. Similarly, do this for adding A Record.

This is optional but you can do it if you want.

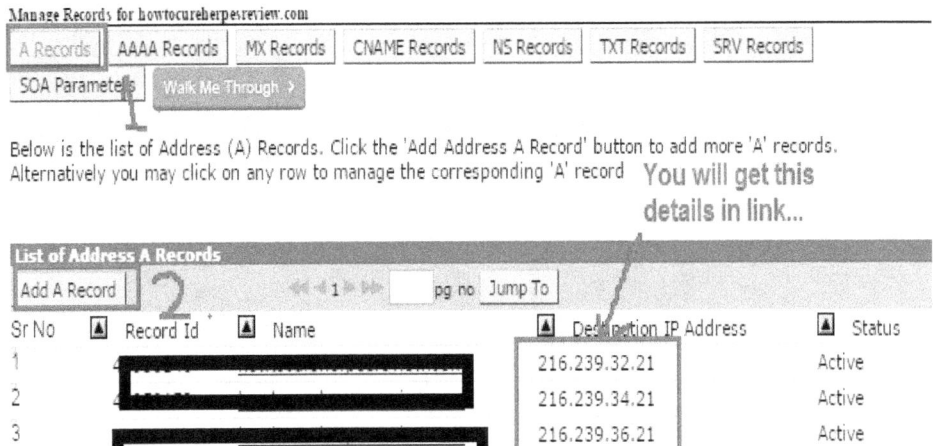

After you complete these steps, wait for an hour then check your status for Active. Now you have to complete a final step in mapping.

Go to your Bloggers blog dashboard. Click on "setting" then click on "Set up third party URL" as shown below.

This will take you to the following screen. Enter your own domain name you just registered and click save button. And you have done it.

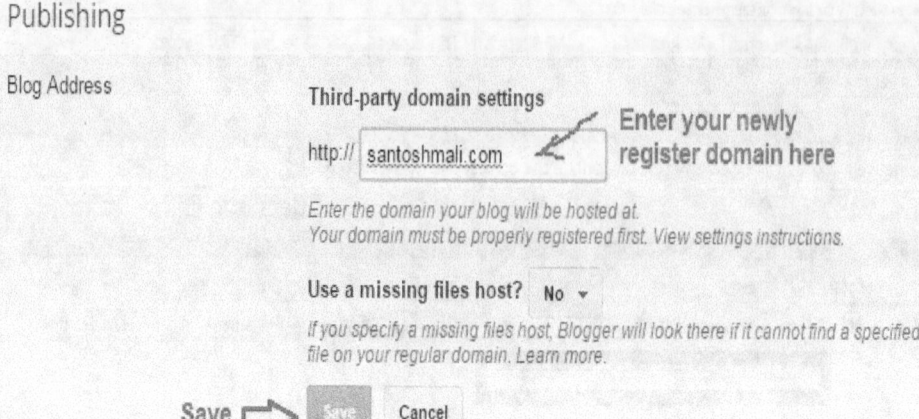

**Congratulation**, you have successfully created a Blogger account. You have got one free blog or if you have mapped your own domain then you have got a personal .com domain that will more appeal to your followers and help to build trust in you.

In this way you can create unlimited Bloggers Blog on any topic you want. This is simple, isn't it?

The MEAT of any blog or website is the unique, quality and engaging contents. Google and other search engines love this MEAT and can award you with high quality free visitors (ready to buy or take action) to your blogs for life.

In fact, it will make you lots of money over the time for FREE. Start adding quality content to your blog. I will not go in details for how to add content to blog. It is quite easy and simple anyone can do it.

Just go to dashboard, click New Post or Page...

Then write what you want to tell to the world, add pictures and links in content, edit if not happy, do proofreading and finally PUBLISH it to the WORLD.

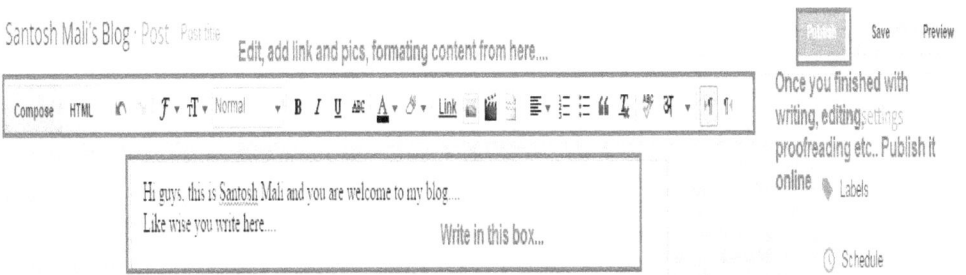

Add more quality content to your blog, edit or update it for your visitors.

You have done the lots of hard work at this point. Friends, you need a Kit-Kat break and you deserve for it.

In the following sections we will discuss how to monetize your blog content and make some extra money for living...

See you in next section...

Hi friends, welcome in this section of how to monetize your blog for money.

In the previous section you have successfully created a personal blog and added some quality contents and might see some of the people are already visited to your blog. Check your statistic in blog dashboard.

There are many ways or methods to monetize your blog and make money from internet. The most common and widely accepted method to make money on the internet is **Affiliate Marketing**. Affiliate marketing is most popular among all of the other methods.

**What is Affiliate Marketing?**

Affiliate marketing works by signing up a website of an internet business as an affiliate to advertise for them. You simply won't be really marketing their product or services; however, you just need to pre-sell the product or services.

This means that if you register as an affiliate of an internet business and add some banners to your blog, your blog becomes just like a hoarding or signboard or an advertising house.

In contrast to billboards, internet businesses won't pay you to post their links or banners on the blog; they're going to pay you a commission only if an online visitor from your blog clicks the affiliate link or banner and buy the product or services an internet business is providing.

So, in affiliate marketing you actually make money from percentage commissions when a visitor you sent to an internet business actually buys the product or join their services. An internet business then pays you a percentage commission of that product or service to help them getting a quality customer.

Visit Here To Know Benefits of Affiliate Marketing

http://www.freefinancialfreedom.com/benefits-being-affiliate-marketer-online/

## How Much Money Can You Make in Affiliate Marketing?

For an example, you get 1,000 clicks in a month (33 clicks per day) to your blog. This is quite feasible and you even get more per month as you continuously adding quality and engaging content on your blog.

Let's assume that out of these 1,000 clicks, you get a 20% click-through rate on your affiliate links or banners on your blog.

So 1,000 x 0.20 = **200 affiliate clicks per month.**

**Case-1:** If only 2% out of that 200 clicks end up buying what you promote, you will get 4 sales.

**Case-2:** If only 5% out of that 200 clicks end up buying what you promote, you will get 10 sales.

**Case-3:** If your blog traffic is high quality you can get 10% out of that 200 clicks end up buying what you promote, you will get 20 sales.

And suppose you are promoting a product or service that pays $30 commission per sale (there are some products that pay even $100 commission per sale). You will earn $120 in Case-1, $300 in Case-2 and $600 in Case-3. And that is good amount as NEWBIE, isn't it?

## Adding Affiliate Links and Banners to Blog

I hope, you got the idea of affiliate marketing and how much can you make as an affiliate marketer. Now we will see how to add affiliate links and banners to your Blogger blog.
There are many Affiliate Programs over the internet that act as a middle-man between the affiliates like us and the internet businesses. You need to join

these Affiliate Programs rather than joining individual businesses.

Affiliate Programs are reliable and free to join. Here are some of the common Affiliate Networks you can join,

(1) Amazon Associate: Sell products from Amazon
(2) ClickBank: Famous for digital products
(3) Commission Junction: Famous for Physical products. But there are some digital products too.
(3) ShareASale
(4) LinkShare

Join one more from above programs as you wish.

Let's consider you join in ClickBank. Once you logged in to your ClickBank account, click on "Marketplace" tab...

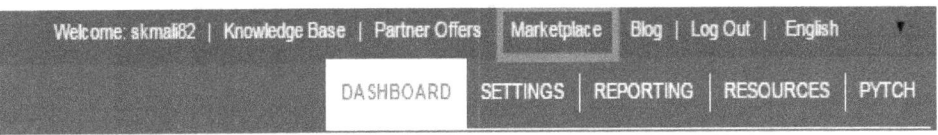

Then you will be taken to following window. There are many niches available to choose from. Just choose your niche from these categories and select the popular product related to your niche.

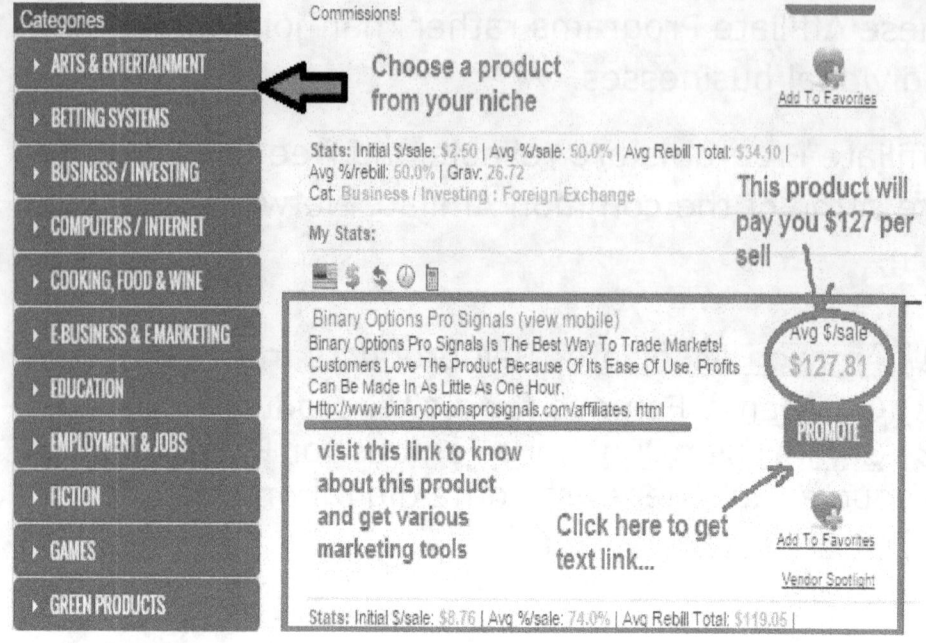

Select a product that has more than 30 gravity rating. High gravity rating means that product is very popular and can be selling easily.

Visit the link in description to know more about the product and to get various marketing material such as text links, banners, videos etc...

Click on "PROMOTE" button. It will pop up the following window to get a specially coded text link for adding on your blog.

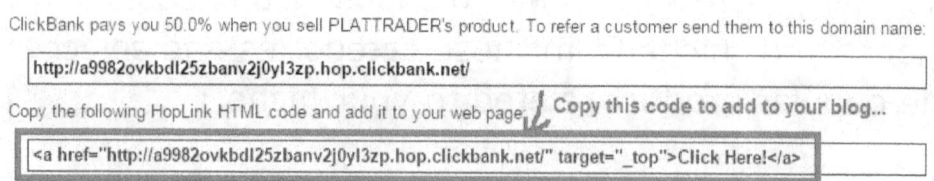

Copy the entire code highlighted in blue and save it in notepad so you can use it whenever you want.

Now head over to your Blog dashboard. Open a post or a page in edit mode in which you want to add this affiliate product link.

Follow these steps 1 to 4 and publish or update your post/page.

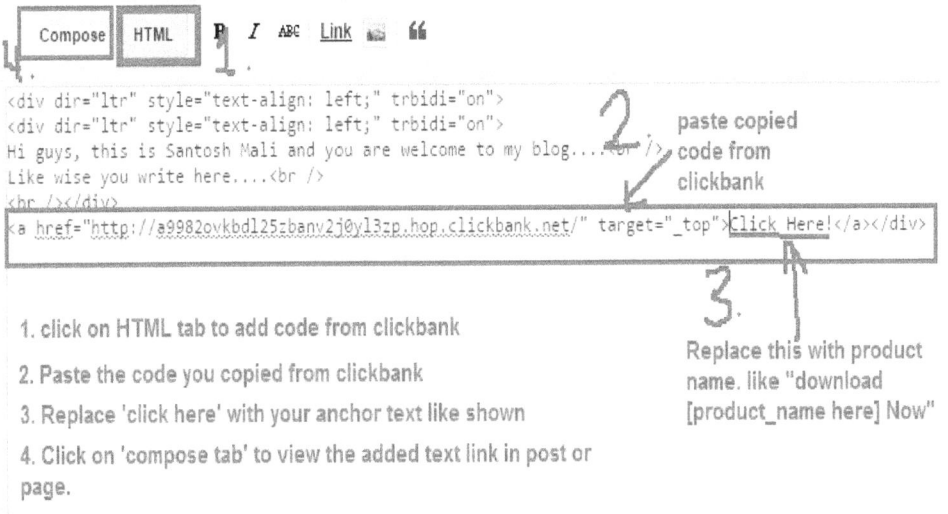

1. click on HTML tab to add code from clickbank
2. Paste the code you copied from clickbank
3. Replace 'click here' with your anchor text like shown
4. Click on 'compose tab' to view the added text link in post or page.

Replace this with product name. like "download [product_name here] Now"

Your affiliate link will look like this.

Hi guys, this is Santosh Mali and you are welcome to my blog....
Like wise you write here....

"download [product_name here] Now"!

Your affiliate link for that product

So make sure your Anchor text (i.e. keywords or phrase in place of [Click Here]) is eye catchy and make people to click on it.

Anyone click on this link and buys this product, you will get commission as mentioned in the product description.

For adding affiliate links, banners or anything else in your Blogger blog sidebar, follow these steps.

Click on "Layout" on dashboard. This will open up the following window.

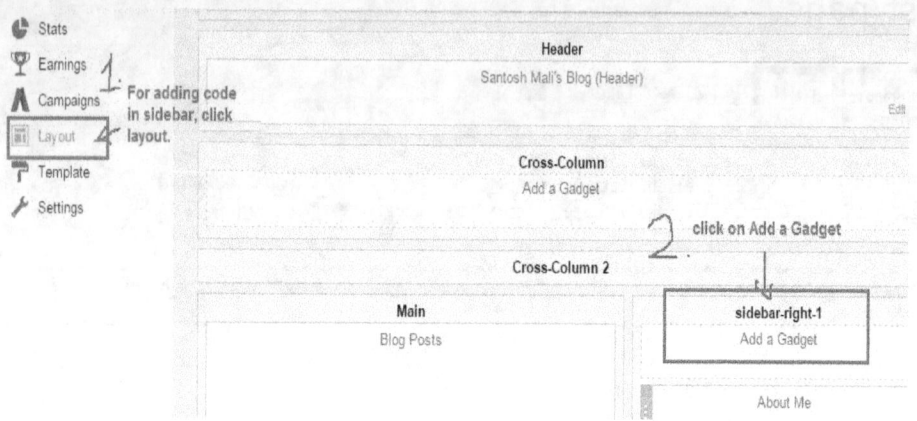

Click on "Add a Gadget" link as shown above.

A new pop-up window will be open. Choose the HTML/Java Script Gadget from the list.

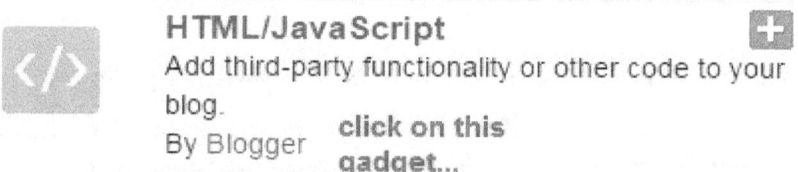

Now paste your copied HTML code or affiliate link from ClickBank or any other Affiliate Program in this window and save it.

## Configure HTML/JavaScript

Title

|                                              |
| -------------------------------------------- |

Content                                    **b** *i* 🈁 66 | Rich Text

Paste HTML
code you copied
from clickbank
here in this box

finally save it

**Save**    Cancel        Back

And you have done with adding your affiliate links in post content and sidebar gadgets.

Follow the similar procedure for adding affiliate text links or banners to your Google blog from any Affiliate Program you joined.

You can ask for help in this regards. I will more than happy to help you.

In the next section I am going to show you another popular blog monetizing method that you will happy to integrate on your blog.

Many bloggers and affiliate marketers to whom I know are using this strategy to make tons of money on the internet.

Before we proceed to next section, add at least one or two quality and engaging post to your blog today.

This will be helpful to you to get started in the following sections.

Do the blogging regularly and you will see increase in your blog visitors.

See you in the next section...

We have learned what affiliate marketing is and why it is one of the most popular monetizing methods among super bloggers. We have also seen some of its benefits in previous chapter. I also like affiliate marketing for my website.

In this section I am going to show you the second profitable monetizing method for your blog. And this method is creating your own product or training eBooks related to your niche.

For example, if your blog niche is about Weight Loss and health, create an eBook or training related to this niche. If your niche is all about Home Business or affiliate/internet marketing, create an eBook or training on that topic and so on.

**Creating your own eBook has many advantages.**

1. You can sell it on personal blog for any price you would like to charge.

2. You can sell it on high traffic website like Amazon, eBay and many other book selling websites.
3. You keep all money for yourself.
4. You can give it away free for building subscriber to your mailing list. Building huge mailing list is highly beneficial for future business. You might have heard this "Money Is in the List".
5. You can build your brand by creating various eBook related to your niche. It will help you build authorship online and people may trust you more and have a stronger relationship.
6. You create it once and it will pay you for life.
7. It is a digital product. So you need not any publisher and print it, you can be directly list for selling online.
8. It doesn't require any physical space to store it. Your computer hard drive is just you need.

## Creating an eBook for Blog and Amazon Kindle

Creating an eBooks is easy as writing a blog. If you have sound knowledge and experience in your niche, you can create as many eBooks as you wish. You don't have to write 10,000+ words eBook, 4,000 to 5,000 words eBook is enough to sell online.

If you don't have any ideas about eBook topics in your niches, there are many websites over the internet that allows you to download free PLR

(Private Label Rights) eBooks on almost any topic you want to write about.

Please don't upload PLR eBook as it is for selling online. Because, PLR eBooks are free to download online. Many people may download the same PLR eBook for them too.

You just need to refer it for getting some ideas to write about and if you wish you can re-write some of the chapters in your own words. You can add your personal experience to make it strong and valuable.

If you know how to create an eBook in MS Word program that is good. But if you don't, download this Kindle eBook ready template here [https://www.dropbox.com/s/7dvhmemwit98e3s/Kindle%20Template.docx] and start building your eBook right now.

Remember: Don't delete any part of this template. You need to update eBook title, sub-title if any, Author and copy-paste your eBook contents in this template. Don't change even the font size.

So when you are finished with copying and pasting the content in Word template and have changed the titles to whatever your chapter titles are, head over to the Table of Contents, right click and select "Update Field" as shown in picture below and save it in your hard-drive.

# Table of Contents

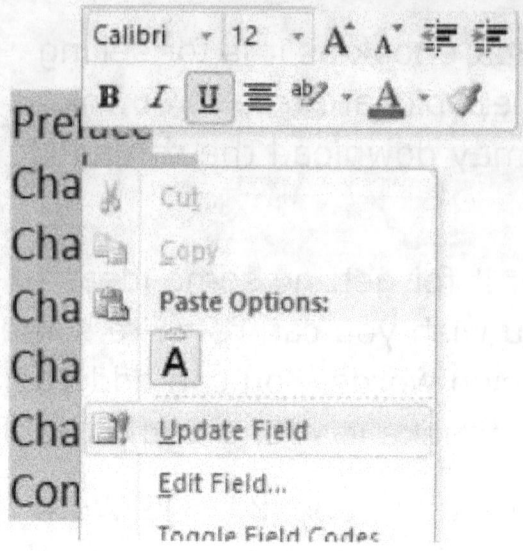

Congratulation, you have finished your first eBook for your blog and selling it on Amazon Kindle.

## It's Time to add Your eBook on Amazon

Visit this link to join Amazon Kindle here, it is free. http://kdp.amazon.com

When you log in to Amazon kindle account, you will take to the "Bookshelf" dashboard where you can add an eBook.

Just click on "Add New Title" button over there as shown.

Introducing Kindle Countdown Deals
A new KDP Select book promotion tool to hel
› Learn More

Add new title ⟵ Click here to add new eBook

Once you click on this button, you will be brought to a page where you will have to enter the details of you eBook like title, sub-title, author name, description, book contributors etc… Just fill out everything possible there.

Next you will be asking for eBook cover. You have two options here, you can choose an image from your computer or you can design it from their gallery.

You can play with this part but don't waste too much time on creating cover. Choose something related to your eBook content.

## 4. Upload or Create a Book Cover

Upload an existing cover, or design a high-quality cover with Cover Creator. (optio

No Cover Available

I have a book cover designed and ready to upload
Please read our Cover guidelines

Browse for image...     ⇐ Upload from computer

OR

I want to design a cover using the Cover Creator (beta).

Launch Cover Creator beta     ⇐ Design online

If you have one best image for your eBook in your hard-drive, choose first option else go for second option and design your beautiful eBook cover from their image gallery.

Now go to next step... uploading your eBook Word Document which you have created in eBook template.

## 5. Upload Your Book File

Select a digital rights management (DRM) option:

○  Enable digital rights management
◉  Do not enable digital rights management

Book content file:

Browse     ⇐

Make sure "Do Not Enable Digital Rights Management" is selected, and then click on the "Browse" button to upload your eBook.

Once you done uploading your eBook, you will be brought to the page where you can select the rights and set the price for your eBook. You will be asked to "Verify Your Publishing Territories". Make sure you choose it to "Worldwide Rights".

Next you have to select your royalty. Choose your royalty to 70% and set the price you want. Recommended to set at lowest price $2.99 and check out how many downloads you get.

More download means your eBook is popular and you can make slight increment in price and check for download again. Make small increments in price rather than increasing $2 or $5 at a time.

Now you are on the last stage of publishing your eBook. Select the box that says you have all the rights necessary to publish the book and that you are agreeing to the TOS. Now click "Save and publish".

Great job, you have successfully listed your brand new eBook on Amazon Kindle for people to download. It may take 24 hrs to review and approve your eBook by Amazon.

So hold tight and check an email from Amazon that your eBook is approved and ready to download.

Once your eBook is approved, you may see the results by the next day.

## How much can you earn from an eBook?

Let's assume that you create 2 eBook per month. Actually you can create more, but for simplicity we will consider only 2 eBook.

So you will have total 24 eBook at the end of year. Amazon's KDP (Kindle Direct Publishing) is a great platform for selling eBooks. The least price to sell in KDP is $2.99.

If you charge the least price of $2.99 and set your royalty to 70%, on this price you will get around $2 per sale. Consider you have listed 24 eBooks for sell on KDP. If each eBook is downloaded twice per day, you will have;

**24*2= 48** download per day which in turns will make you **48*$2 = $96 per day**. So your monthly income will be **$96*30 = $2880**. How much for YEAR......?

Remember this income is only from Amazon. In addition to that your blog is also making you sell of your eBooks and that is just EXTRA money to you.

You can multiply this income by creating more eBooks and increasing your least price by a $1 or $2. But increasing price can reduces the rate of download. So you might consider increasing the number of eBooks rather than its price.

**REMEMBER THIS IS AN EXAMPLE ONLY. YOU CAN EVEN MAKE MORE OR LESS DEPENDING ON YOUR READER. IF YOU HAVE EYE CATCHING TITLE OR COVER, YOU CAN SELL MORE... IT'S ONLY DEPENDS ON READER.**

So enjoy your eBook income from Amazon Kindle.

In next section I will show you how to sell your eBook on your personal Blog.

Add some new posts to your blog before seeing you in the next section.

Done?

Ok, see you in the next section...

Welcome back. In previous section, you have seen how to create an eBook to sell online. And I guess you already have created one eBook and uploaded to Amazon Kindle, Right?

If not, then I request to take action on what you have learned at this point.

So, let's start selling your eBook on personal blog...

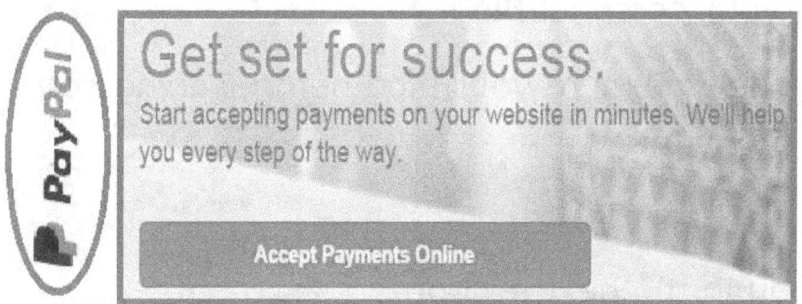

Get set for success.

Start accepting payments on your website in minutes. We'll help you every step of the way.

Accept Payments Online

10.7 million buyers are actively using PayPal in Asia Pacific.

For selling an eBook on your blog, you need 3 things to be ready with you.

### #1: Sales Page

Create one interesting and informative sale page about your eBook on your blog. List all the benefits of your eBook and explain to your visitors why they need to download or buy this eBook.

If you don't have any ideas about creating effective sale page, just go to Google and type "**Your Niche name + sample sale page**". Review the sample pages and edit it according to your eBook contents.

You know how to create a page in Blogger blog and publish it, right?

Ok, create one sales page for your eBook and save draft. Don't publish yet.

#### #2: Getting Your Auto eBook Downloads URL

Setting up an automatic sale funnel for your eBook is important. If you do it correctly, you don't have to take action yourself to send eBook manually when someone buys your eBook.

First upon create a free account here www.dropbox.com and log in.

Once you logged in to Dropbox account, **click on file icon** as shown in below image and follow the onscreen guideline to upload your **eBook in .PDF** format.

Once you upload your eBook to Dropbox, Hover your mouse on eBook name and click on "share".

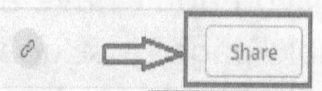

You will be brought to the following window.

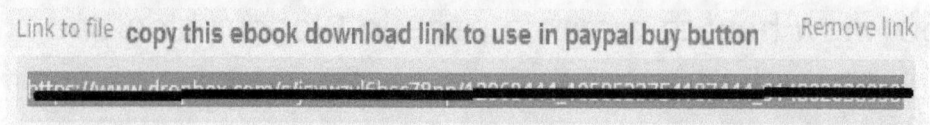

This is your **eBook download URL**. Copy this complete URL and save it in notepad. You will need this URL while setting up payment processor.

### # 3: Setting up eBook Payment Processor

For selling your eBook on blog you need to set up a payment processor. There are many options but PayPal Is best. So let's set up a payment processor and create a Buy Button for your eBook...

First, create a free account at www.paypal.com here.

Once you login to your PayPal account, click on "Profile".

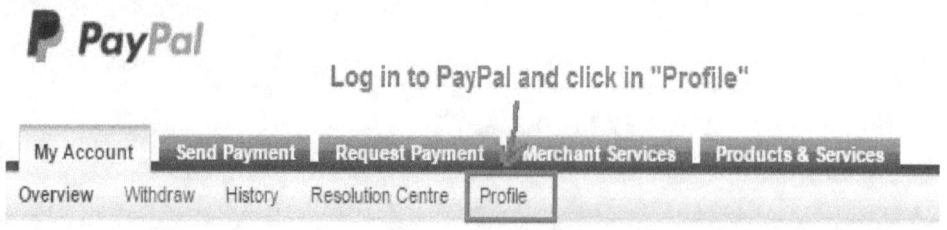

It will bring you to the following window:

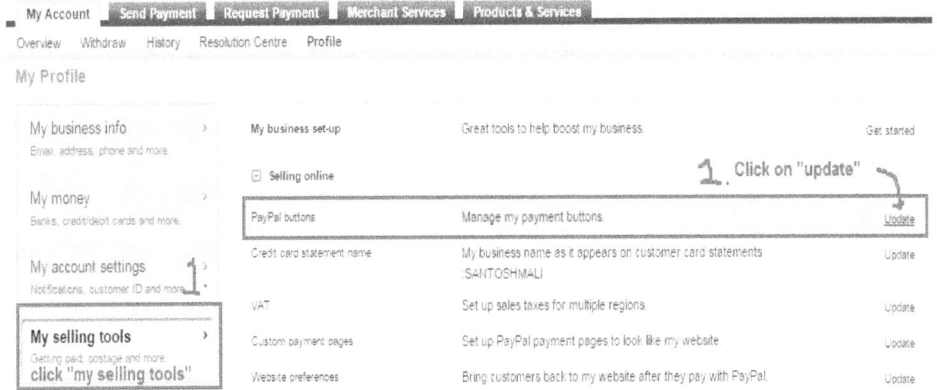

Click on "My selling tools" and then click on PayPal buttons "Update" link.

You will see the following window…

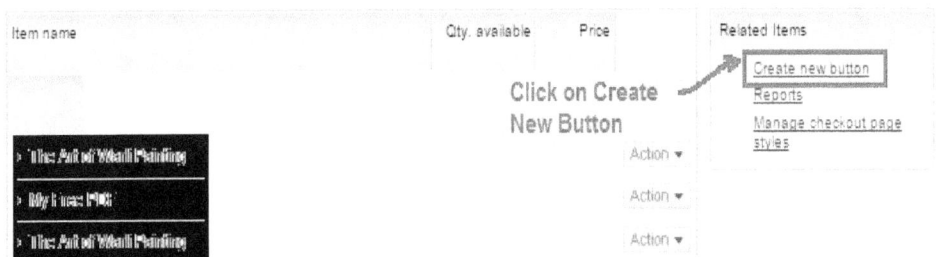

Click on "Create new button". You will get to this window to create your new buy button.

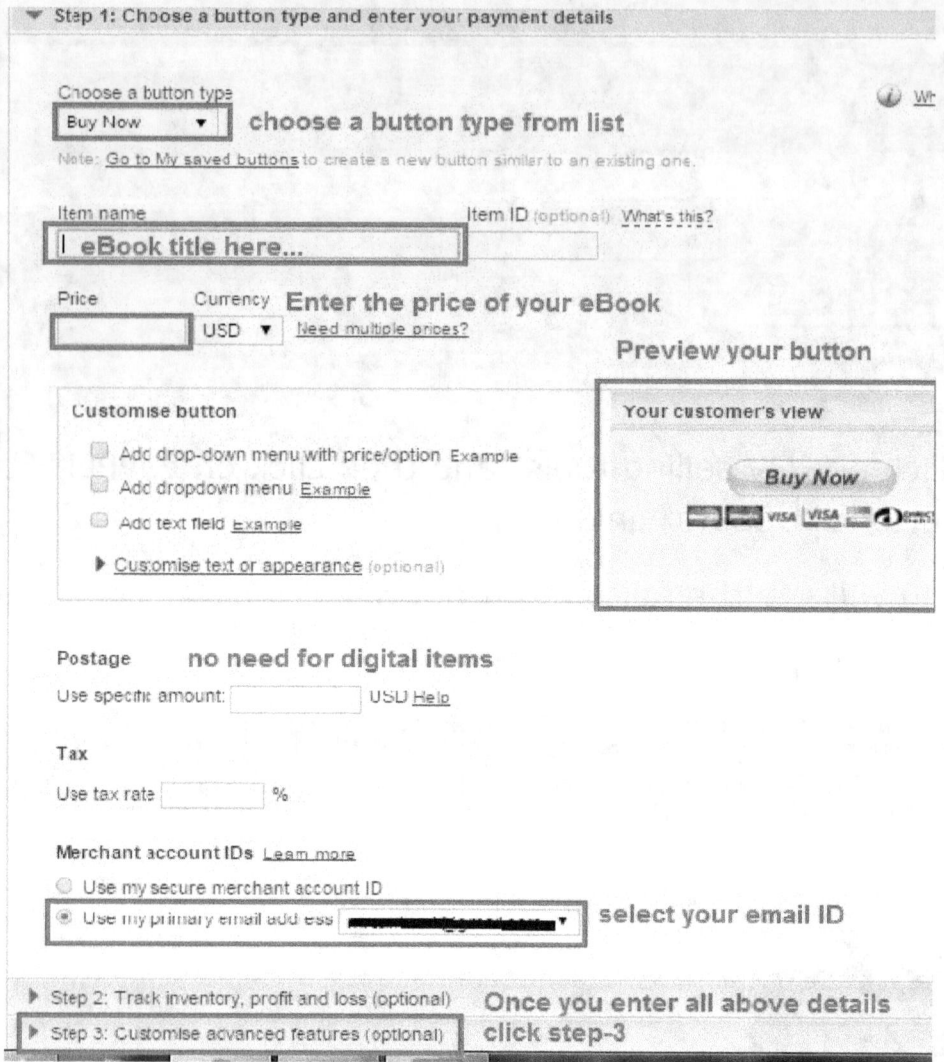

Choose a button type from dropdown list. You can see its preview how it will be look online to your customers.

Enter your eBook title in the box provided and set the price you want to charge for this eBook.

Next, select your email Id and click on "Step 3: Customer advance feature".

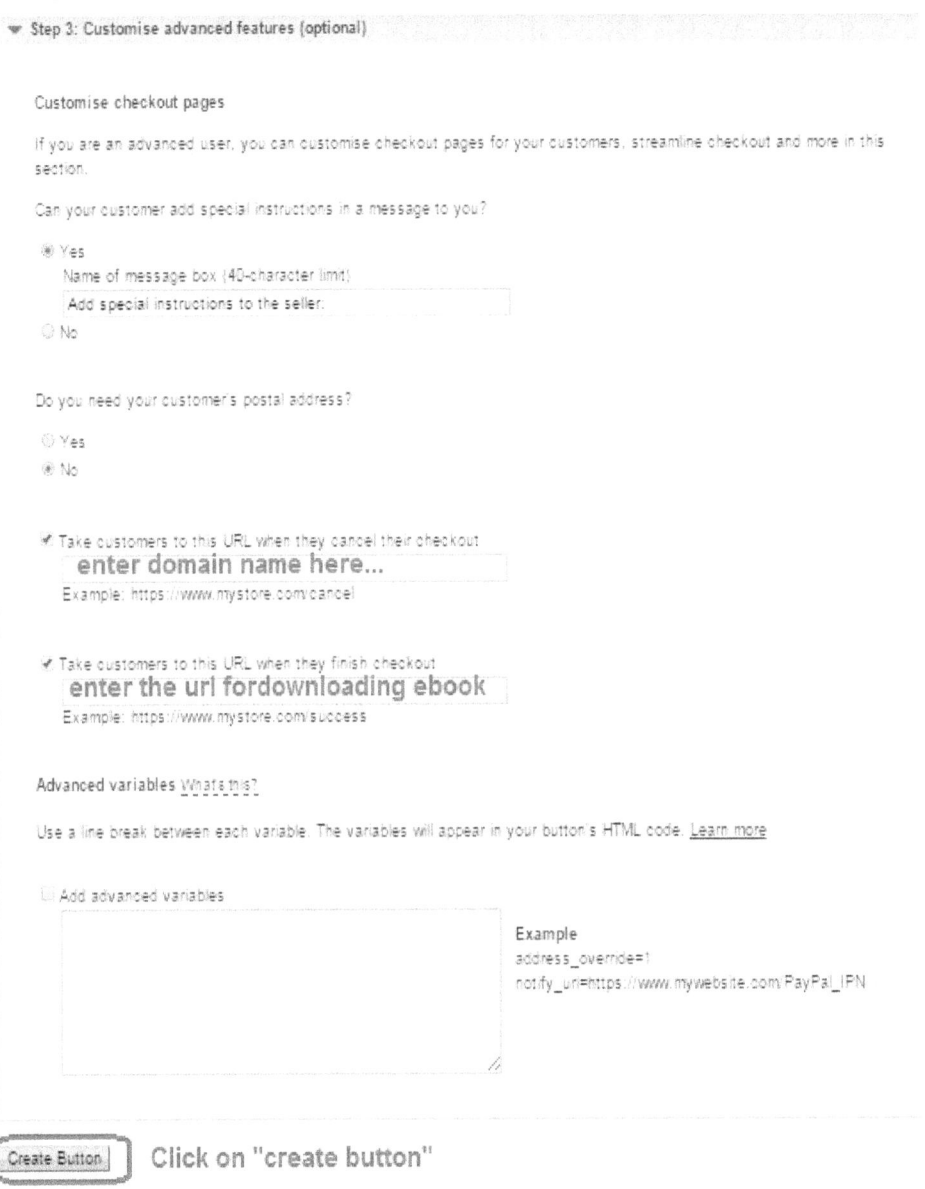

Customise checkout pages

If you are an advanced user, you can customise checkout pages for your customers, streamline checkout and more in this section.

Can your customer add special instructions in a message to you?

⦿ Yes

Name of message box (40-character limit)

Add special instructions to the seller.

◯ No

Do you need your customer's postal address?

◯ Yes

⦿ No

☑ Take customers to this URL when they cancel their checkout

enter domain name here...

Example: https://www.mystore.com/cancel

☑ Take customers to this URL when they finish checkout

enter the url fordownloading ebook

Example: https://www.mystore.com/success

Advanced variables What's this?

Use a line break between each variable. The variables will appear in your button's HTML code. Learn more

☐ Add advanced variables

Example
address_override=1
notify_url=https://www.mywebsite.com/PayPal_IPN

Create Button  Click on "create button"

**Enter your blog URL** or another **affiliate link** or **link to other eBooks** in take customer to this URL when they cancel checkout box.

Enter **eBook Download URL** that you have created and copied from Dropbox (Did you remember?) in take customer to this URL when they finish checkout box. As shown in above image.

Finally, click on "Create Button" and you will be landed on this page.

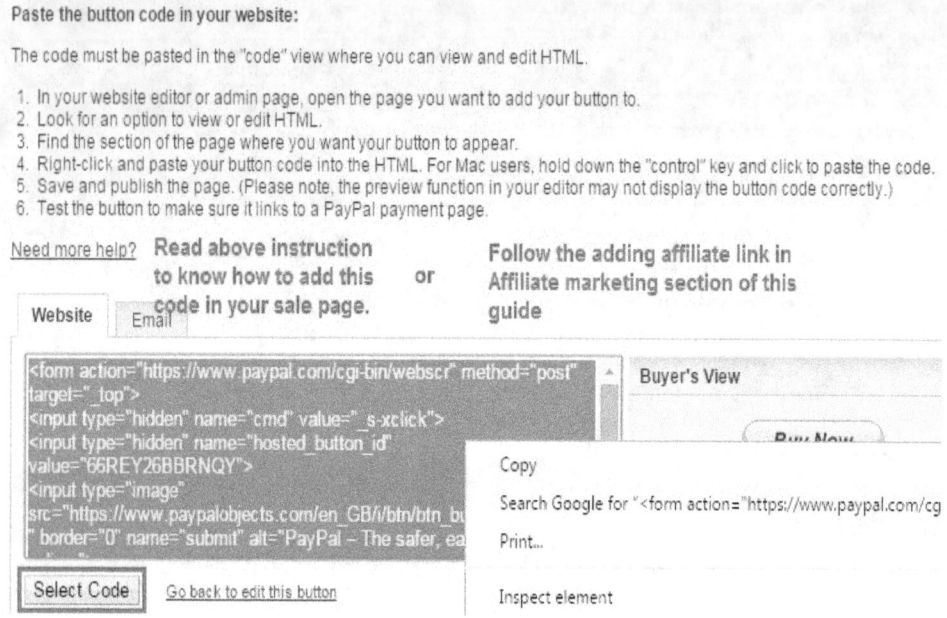

Read the instruction there on how to add this button code in your eBook sale page or just follow the steps you have learned in Affiliate Marketing section on how to add affiliate links on posts or pages.

Then click on "Select Code" button. Right click on highlighted area and copy this code.

You always need to save these codes or Affiliate links in Notepad because you often need it.

Add this "PayPal Payment Processor Code" into your sales page wherever you want and **PUBLISH** your sales page.

*Once you published it, go and check it as a customer to confirm everything is fine and working automatically.*

In this way, create as many eBook as you wish and sell it on your blog.

**Note: You need to follow this procedure for each and every eBook you creates. For each eBook you need to create a separate PayPal button and get a separate download URL.**

In the next section, I am going to introduce you with one more blog monetizing method.

I hope, you are continuously adding contents to your blog and at this point you have at least 8 to 10 blog posts on your blog and may get some visitors regularly.

This will help you getting started in next blog monetizing method.

If have not that much posts, try adding some new blog posts. If you already have then,

See you in the next section...

In previous sections we have learned various blog monetizing methods like affiliate marketing, creating a digital product like an eBook for Amazon and your blog, right?

In this section I am going to show you yet another effective blog monetizing method to add some extra boost in your blog income and that is Google AdSense Program.

## What Is Google AdSense Program?

The Google AdSense Program for Your Website

Small Investment Options
Invest in best SIP plans in just 2 Mins & avail high returns.

Ads by Google

Did you see such ads all over the internet? Yes, these are Google ads from which they makes thousands of millions of dollar per month.

You might know Google's AdWard program. Google sell traffic to advertisers through this advertising program. Advertisers pay Google to advertise or display their business ads on Google. And Google offer blog or website owners to advertise these ads on their blog through the Google AdSense Program.

Google AdSense is a PPC (Pay per Click) program in which you become partner with Google to advertise

AdWard ads on your blog. When your blog visitors click on these AdSense ads, **you will get paid from Google for each and every click your visitors make unlike as in affiliate marketing.**

In Google AdSense, you don't need to wait for clicker to buy from your ads. Once a visitor click on Google ads on your blog, you get paid from Google whether that visitor buy or not from that advertiser does not matter.

**What you need to join Google AdSense Program?**

In order to join this program, first Google requires you to have an active, running blog or website before approving a new AdSense account. Make sure you have at least 10 articles on your blog and getting some visitors to your blog.

Once your account is approved, you can add the code into any site that meets their content guidelines.

Google will not approve your application if your blog contents fall into one or more of the following categories.

- Adult content
- Content that advocates against an individual, group, or organization
- Copyrighted material

- Drug, alcohol, and tobacco-related content
- Hacking and cracking content
- Sites that offer compensation programs ("pay-to" sites)
- Sites that use Google Brand features
- Violent contents
- Weapon-related content

If you meet all of the above conditions, join here
https://www.google.com/adsense/signup

OR follow these steps...

**Head over to your blog dashboard.**

**Click on "Earning" and then "Sign up for AdSense".**

# Welcome to AdSense

Sign in to your Google Account or create a new one to sign up for AdSense. Which AdSense account.

If you're already an AdSense publisher, you must sign in with the Google Account that you use

If you already have Adsense account click on sign in, else create new account with your existing Gmail ID.

 Create account

If you already have AdSense account**, click on "Sign in" else "Create new account".** Follow the steps...

Congratulations!
The AdSense widget has been added to your blog template.
Press Continue to customise your AdSense settings.

CONTINUE          Once you registered successfully, you will see
                  this message. Click on Continue...

**Congratulations,** you have created AdSense account. Click on "Continue" button. You will be bringing to the following window.

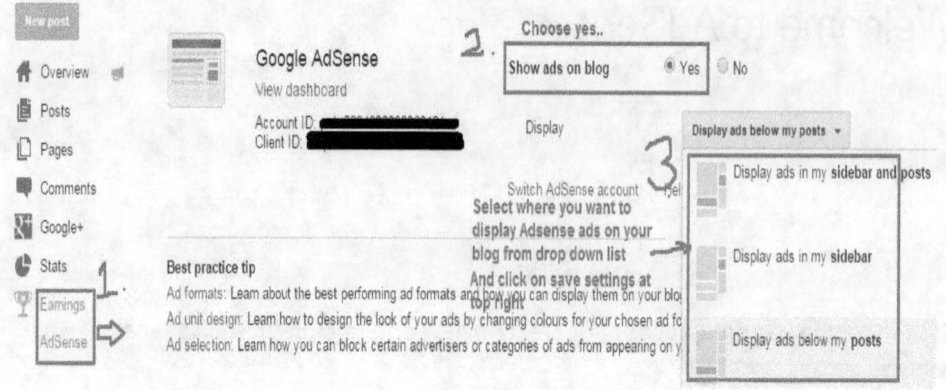

Select "Yes" then choose where to display AdSense ads on your blog from dropdown list.

Selecting first option will show ads on the sidebar and below the posts.

Selecting second option will show ads on sidebar only and the third option will show ads below the post only.

If you want to add more AdSense ads on your blog, follow these steps....

First click on "Layout" link in dashboard >> Choose in layout where you want to put an ads i.e. in sidebar, header or in footer section >> click on "Get a Gadget" link in that section >> Choose AdSense Gadget.

**AdSense**
Earn revenue by displaying relevant ads on your blog.
By Blogger

**HTML/JavaScript**
Add third-party functionality or other code to your blog.
By Blogger

Google allows to us to show maximum of 3 AdSense ads per page.

**REMEMBER**: You need to adhere to Google AdSense Policy [https://support.google.com/adsense/answer/23921?hl=en&ref_topic=1261918] and never click on AdSense ads on your blog even if for testing purpose. If you do so, your account will be suspended and you will never allow joining again.

So make it sure you don't click on AdSense ads on your blog. Google have a strong monitoring on their ads. Don't try to cheat them, OK?

## How much money can you make from AdSense?

Let's say an advertiser pay $1 per click to Google. Google generally pay their partner like us around 60% per click. So you will get around $1*60% = $0.6 per click.

If your blog generates minimum of 50 click per day on AdSense ads, you get $0.6 * 50 = $30 per day.

Try to get 100 clicks per day and easily make $60 per day i.e. $1800 extra per month.

Try to get 500 clicks per day and make $300 per day and $9000 per month.

Here you need more visitors to make big money. Add more content, get more visitors and in turns make MORE MONEY.

You have learned what you need to get started online. It's time to closing this book.

# Thanking You!

First upon let me thank you for reading this book and taking action on what you have learned in this book.

Let me review in brief what you have accomplished at this point.

In first section, you learned what Google Blogger platform is and you have created a free blog using it.

Then, in next sections you learned about how to monetize your blog using affiliate marketing, creating own products like an eBooks. And we have also learned that how to sell these eBooks on Amazon Kindle to get additional profit.

You also learned how to sell these eBooks on your blog using PayPal payment processor.

I hope you loved the last section about Google AdSense Program and might already get approved by Google.

All the blog monetizing methods I covered in this book are completely free of cost and I guess that you didn't require a penny if you don't want to map your own domain with blogger account.

Overall I hope you enjoyed reading this guide and wanted to take serious action for your Financial Freedom in coming days.

If you forget to download your FREE GIFT, here is the link again, Go and download.
http://freefinancialfreedom.com/download-free-gift.html

This Free Gift is something you can't afford to miss!

Join my list here...to know more about INCOME FORMULA!

**http://freefinancialfreedom.com/income-formula**

Thanks again for purchasing this book and for valuable time spent with me!

If you need help, I am here.
support@freefinancialfreedom.com or simply sent IM on **Facebook** and Twitter feeds.

*Santosh mali*

-----------------------------------------------------